Pre-Intermediate

Just

Listening and Speaking

For class or self-study

Ana Acavedo
Carol Lethaby
Jeremy Harmer
with Cheryl Pelteret

D0121057

Marshall Cavendish
Education

© 2007 Marshall Cavendish Education

First published 2007 by Marshall Cavendish Education
Marshall Cavendish is a member of the Times Publishing Group

ISBN (10-digit) 0 462 00777 4
     (13-digit) 978 04620 00777 9

Marshall Cavendish Education
119 Wardour Street
London W1F 0UW

Designed by Hart McLeod, Cambridge
Illustrations by Jo Taylor, Yane Christiansen, Francis Fung, Rory Walker,
Valeryia Steadman, Tim Oliver

Printed and bound by Times Offset (M) Sdn Bhd

Contents

Introduction

For the student

Just Listening and Speaking is part of an integrated series of books designed for you to study on your own, or together with other students and a teacher. It will help you improve your listening and speaking skills in English.

We have chosen the listening extracts and speaking tasks carefully to offer an interesting and challenging mix of topics and activities. With the listening extracts there are exercises to help you understand them and learn new language from them. In the speaking sections we help you do the tasks successfully. You can also listen to other people doing the same tasks. From pages 54 – 67 you have also got a number of pronunciation exercises to help you with difficult sounds and other pronunciation items.

There is an accompanying CD with all the listening extracts and speaking examples. You will find an audioscript at the back of the book.

When you see this symbol ( ) it means that the answers to the exercises are in the answer key which starts on page 83. You can check your answers there.

We are confident that this book will help you become a better listener and speaker of English. Enjoy using it!

For the teacher

The *Just* series is a flexible set of teaching materials that can be used on their own, or in any combination, or as a set to form a complete integrated course. The *Just* series has been written and designed using a consistent methodological approach that allows the books to be used easily together. Each book in the series specialises in either language skills or aspects of the English language. It can be used either in class or by students working on their own. The listening extracts (in Part A of each Unit) include stories, dialogues, radio programmes and joke-telling. The speaking tasks (in Part B of each Unit) involve taking part in interviews, role-playing, and stimulating debates.

From page 54 there are pronunciation exercises on different sounds, on stress and on intonation.

All the listening extracts and pronunciation exercises are on the accompanying CD together with example versions of the speaking tasks. There is an audioscript at the back of the book, together with a comprehensive answer key where students can check their work.

We are confident that you will find this book a real asset and that you will also want to try the other books in the series: *Just Reading and Writing*, *Just Vocabulary* and *Just Grammar*.

●● A Listening

About countries

1 Look at this map. What do the countries in red have in common? 🔑

Which 'red' country is the odd one out? Check your answer at the bottom of the page.

· ·

2 Look at the picture. Where are the people from?

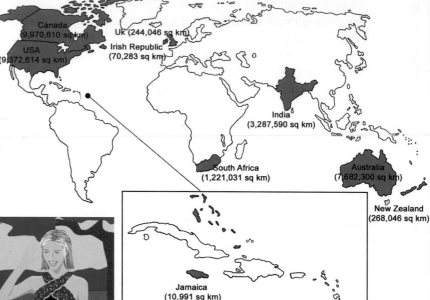

Canada
(9,970,610 sq km)

UK (244,046 sq km)
Irish Republic
(70,283 sq km)

USA
(9,372,614 sq km)

India
(3,287,590 sq km)

South Africa
(1,221,031 sq km)

Australia
(7,682,300 sq km)

New Zealand
(268,046 sq km)

Jamaica
(10,991 sq km)

Sandy   Matt   Wilson   Tessa

🎧 Listen to Track 1 to check your answer.   🔑

· ·

🎧 **3** Read the sentences. Then listen to Track 1 again. Who is each sentence about? The first one is done for you.

a He is from an island in the Caribbean. ......*Wilson*...............

b People in her country speak French or English, or both. ....

c Her city is bigger than the capital of her country. ....

d One in three families in his country speak English and another language. ....

e Reggae comes from his country. ....

f Eighty per cent of the people in his country live on the coast. ....

g Her country is in Great Britain but she is not English. ....

h His country is famous for its beaches and its mountains. ....   🔑

4 Listen to Track 1 again and answer the questions.

   a How do Australians say 'Good morning'?

   ....

   b What is another way of saying 'one in three'?

   ....

   c Name two open air activities Australians enjoy.

   ....

   d What three countries make up Great Britain?

   ....

   e What language do some people speak in Scotland?

   ....

   f What's the capital of Scotland?

   ....

   g Name two of Canada's natural features.

   ....

   h What are the most popular sports in Canada?

   ....

   i What is the capital of Jamaica?

   ....

   j What two things make Jamaica popular with tourists?

   ....

5 Read the text and listen to Track 2. Circle the word you hear for each letter. The first one is done for you.

> Hi! I'm Tessa, from Montreal, in Quebec. Quebec is in the (a) *east* / *west* / *south* of Canada. Most (b) *people* / *Americans* / *Canadians* speak the two official languages, French and English. Canada is a (c) *big* / *huge* / *large* country, the second largest in the world actually. In Canada you can find (d) *everything* / *anything* / *nothing*. Do you like big (e) *places* / *cities* / *countries*? We have really exciting ones, like Montreal and Toronto. Do you like mountains? We have (f) *two* / *lots* / *some* too. (g) *Water* / *Winter* sports are very popular. It is very cold in winter, but I like summer better. It's warm and we go and swim in the lakes.

6 Listen to Track 3 and complete the table. Then guess the name of the country.

Where it is:	
Capital:	
Languages:	
Most popular sports:	
Interesting information:	

••• B Speaking

Discussing holidays

1 Complete the dialogue with your own ideas. Follow the instructions in *italics*.

YOUR FRIEND: Where shall we go for our holiday this year?

YOU: How about (*say a country or place*) .... ?

It's (*say something good*) .... and

the weather is always (*say what it is like*) ....

.... in (*say a holiday

month*) ....

YOUR FRIEND: I'd rather do something more exciting this year. How about an extreme sports holiday in Wales?

YOU: I prefer (*say what you like doing in the place you have suggested*).

.... to waterskiing and canoeing.

YOUR FRIEND: But we do that every year. I'd prefer to do something different this time. It would be nice to go somewhere quieter.

YOU: OK, you win. I admit, (*the place you mentioned earlier*) ....

.... was a bit (*say something negative*)

.... last time. I'd prefer somewhere a

little quieter too, but I'm not into dangerous sports like (*give examples of

dangerous sports you don't like doing*) ....

....

YOUR FRIEND: How about Devon? It'll be warm, and there are some lovely seaside walks.

YOU: That sounds (*say something positive*) ....

....

2 Listen to Track 4. Speak when it is your turn. Use your dialogue.

A Listening

Telling jokes

1 Can you guess the end (the punchline) of the cartoon?

Now listen to Track 5 and check your answer. Did you get the joke?

2 Listen to Track 6. Complete Sam's explanation.

SAM: The control tower wants his (**a**) .... and his (**b**) ...., right? As in 30,000 (**c**) .... But the pilot (**d**) .... height as in 'How (**e**) .... are you?' And the position as in 'Are you (**f**) .... or standing?'

CLAIRE: Yeah. Duh. But it's not funny.

SAM: OK, but I've got another one. Listen. There's this (**g**) .... and she comes into (**h**) ....

CLAIRE: Not (**i**) ...., Sam. I've got (**j**) .... to do.

3 Answer the questions. Listen to Track 5 again if necessary.

a Why is Claire stressed out?

....

b Why does Sam tell her a joke?

....

c Is Claire less stressed now?

....

d Do you think laughter is a good thing when you are stressed?

....

e Claire did not find the joke funny. Did you?

....

4 Complete the following jokes with the endings (punchlines) in the box.

> No, just green hairy monsters with horrible faces.
>
> Don't cry. It's only a joke!
>
> Ten!
>
> Don't worry, Madam. It's not hot.

a Customer: Waiter! Your fingers are in my soup.

Waiter: ....

....

b A: Knock, knock.

B: Who's there?

A: Boo.

B: Boo who?

A: ....

c Patient: Doctor, doctor. I keep seeing green hairy monsters with horrible faces.

Doctor: Have you seen a psychologist?

Patient: ....

....

d Teacher: Jane, if you have ten sweets and Oscar asks you for one and Jackie asks you for two, how many sweets do you have left?

Jane: ....

Listen to Track 7 and check your answers. Tick the jokes you found funny.

- -

5 Look at the pictures and put these sentences in the correct order.

Then listen to Track 8 and check. Did you find the joke funny or not?

- [ ] 'Well,' said the bear, 'at two dollars a glass, I'm not surprised!'
- [ ] Everyone watched as the bear drank.
- [ ] The barman said to the bear, 'We don't get many bears in this bar.'
- [1] A bear walked into a bar one day.
- [ ] When the glass was empty, the bear put it on the table.
- [ ] The bear asked, 'How much is the orange juice?'
- [ ] The people hid under the tables. They were afraid.
- [ ] 'Two dollars.' replied the barman.
- [ ] 'Barman!' said the bear, 'I'd like a glass of orange juice.'
- [ ] Then he got off his chair and walked out the door.

B Speaking
Role-play: giving advice

1 Your friend won a lot of money in a competition. He / She asks you for advice about how to spend it.

Complete the dialogue with your own ideas. Follow the instructions in *italics*.

YOUR FRIEND: I don't know what to do with all this money! Can you give me some advice?

YOU: Well, you should (*suggest something sensible to do with the money*)

....

....

YOUR FRIEND: That's a bit boring, though. What about something fun?

YOU: (*suggest something fun to do with some of the money*)

....

....

YOUR FRIEND: People will think I'm selfish if I don't help someone or something with some of the money.

YOU: (*suggest a way your friend could be helpful to society*)

....

....

YOUR FRIEND: What about all my friends? They'll expect me to give them money too!

YOU: (*suggest something to solve this problem*) ....

....

YOUR FRIEND: What would you like as a gift?

YOU: (*suggest something*) ....

YOUR FRIEND: Thanks for the advice! You've given me lots to think about.

2 Listen to Track 9. Speak when it is your turn. Use your dialogue.

A Listening
Street survey

1 Listen to Track 10. What is the survey about? Write down any words that helped you decide.

....

....

....

2 Listen to Track 10 again. How does each person answer the questions in the survey? Complete the survey.

a
Television: people's preferences

Age: **26**   Sex: **Male**

Q1: How many hours a day do you watch television?
☐ 2 – 4 hours ☐ 4 – 6 hours
☐ more than 6 hours

Q2: What kind of programmes do you prefer to watch?
☐ news ☐ soap operas
☐ documentaries ☐ game shows
☐ sitcoms ☐ sport

Q3: Do you watch other kinds of programmes?
☐ No
☐ Yes (say what) ....

....

b
Television: people's preferences

Age: **19**   Sex: **Female**

Q1: How many hours a day do you watch television?
☐ 2 – 4 hours ☐ 4 – 6 hours
☐ more than 6 hours

Q2: What kind of programmes do you prefer to watch?
☐ news ☐ soap operas
☐ documentaries ☐ game shows
☐ sitcoms ☐ sport

Q3: Do you watch other kinds of programmes?
☐ No
☐ Yes (say what) ....

....

c
Television: people's preferences

Age: .... Sex: ....

Q1: How many hours a day do you watch television?
☐ 2 – 4 hours ☐ 4 – 6 hours
☐ more than 6 hours

Q2: What kind of programmes do you prefer to watch?
☐ news ☐ soap operas
☐ documentaries ☐ game shows
☐ sitcoms ☐ sport

Q3: Do you watch other kinds of programmes?
☐ No
☐ Yes (say what) ....

....

3 Listen to Track 10 again. How did each person answer the following question?

What kind of programme do you prefer to watch?

Man: ....

Woman: ....

4 Now answer the survey for yourself. Who are you more similar to, the man or the woman? What are the similarities and differences?

....

....

5 Listen to Track 10 again and circle the correct answer.

a Why does the man say he will answer the questions, 'if it's quick'?
   1 Because he's in a hurry.
   2 Because he doesn't watch much TV.

b Why does he like documentaries?
   1 Because they're relaxing.
   2 Because they teach you things.

c Why does he say 'Definitely not!' when asked whether he watches soap operas?
   1 He really doesn't like them.
   2 He prefers the news.

d Why is the woman able to watch so much TV?
   1 She doesn't want to miss an episode of her favourite soaps.
   2 She isn't too busy.

e What kind of programmes does she watch?
   1 Soaps.
   2 All kinds.

f Why doesn't she ever miss an episode of *EastEnders*?
   1 Because she hasn't got much to do.
   2 Because it's her favourite.

g Why doesn't she watch documentaries often?
   1 Because they aren't on very often.
   2 Because she prefers to watch programmes that are more fun.

B Speaking

TV: Deciding what to watch

1 Look at the speakers' likes and dislikes in the table.

Then complete the dialogue with suitable words and phrases.
Follow the instructions in *italics*.

	A				B			
Documentaries	☺	☺	☺		☹	☹	☹	☹
Soap operas	☺	☺	☺		☺	☺	☺	☺
The news	☹	☹	☹		☹	☹	☹	
Sitcoms	☺	☺	☺		☹			
Cartoons	☹	☹	☹	☹	☺	☺	☺	
Talk shows	☹	☹			☺			
Reality shows	☺				☹	☹		

A: What's on TV tonight? Is there a good documentary?

B: Oh, no! I (*say how you feel about documentaries*) ....
I'd rather watch a funny cartoon or something. Oh, *Tom and Jerry's* on! (*suggest you watch that together*) ....

....

A: No way. You know I can't stand cartoons. Especially *Tom and Jerry*. I'd like to watch a good sitcom. Is *Dad's Army* on?

B: Oh, that's (*say what you think of that sitcom*) .... !

I really hate it. The news is on in a few minutes.

A: Oh, no, I don't feel like listening to bad news from around the world.

B: (*you feel the same as B I, say so*) ....

(*suggest a talk show*) ....

A: Not if it's that boring old Michael Parkinson. But look! *Big Brother's* started again! Let's watch that.

B: (*say how you feel about reality shows*) ....

(*say that Neighbours is on, and sound pleased*) ....

....

A: Oh, yes! I love that soap, it's my favourite. Right, that's settled then.

Now, what shall we get to eat? ....

2 Listen to Track 11. Speak when it is your turn. Use your dialogue.

Listening

What's my job?

1 Look at the picture. Do you know the game they are playing? What do you think the panel have to do?

Listen to Track 12. Did you guess right?

- -

2 Listen to Track 12 again. Write short yes / no answers to the panel's questions. The first one is done for you.

a Do you work with animals? ......*Yes I do. / No I don't.*......

b Is your occupation dangerous? ....

c Do you work in a special place? ....

d Do you enjoy your job? ....

- -

3 Listen to Track 12 again and answer the questions.

a Name three places where Jason works.

....

....

b Write two words Jason uses to describe his job.

....

....

- -

4 Can you guess Jason's job? Write your guess here.

Jason is a ....

....

Listen to Track 13 to check your answer.

5 Listen to Track 13 again. Complete the dialogue with the words you hear.

PANELLIST A: Sorry. OK. Do you kill the (a) .... you work with?

JASON: Yes! Yes, I have to (b) .... them!

PANELLIST B: Right, I think we've got it! Are you a … Are you one of those

(c) .... who kill rats, or bad insects or

(d) .... like that? Do you kill pests like that? Are you a – what is it?

PANELLIST C: (e) .... controller?

PANELLIST A: Yes, that's it! A pest (f) .... ?

Are you a (g) .... ?

JASON: (h) .... ! I am a pest controller.

6 Read these questions.

☐ Are you a doctor?

☐ Are you in politics?

☐ Do you have to speak other languages in your job?

☐ Do you have to wear a uniform?

☐ Do you help people?

☐ Do you sell anything?

1 Do you travel a lot in your job?

☐ Do you travel by plane?

☐ Would you say you work with people in your job?

7 Now listen to the answers on Track 14.

Put the questions in exercise 6 in the correct order, 1 – 9.

8 Can you guess the job? ....

Listen to Track 15 and see if you were right.

••B Speaking
A mystery job

1 You are describing your mystery job on a radio programme
called *What's my job*?

> You are a camera operator for a film company. You make
> documentaries about different countries, cultures around the
> world, and animals.

2 Complete the dialogue with suitable yes / no answers.
Then listen to Track 16 and speak when it is your turn.

Panellists' questions	Your answers
Do you work with animals?	
Do you work outside?	
Do you wear a special uniform?	
Do you travel in your job?	
Do you need special equipment?	
Is your equipment expensive?	
Does your job make other people happy?	
Do you work alone?	
Does anyone ever see the work you do?	
Do you work with famous people?	
Do you like your job?	
I give up. What do you do?	

A Listening
Team building

1 Look at the picture. Can you guess the right answer? Tick the correct box.

a The people are from an office in the city. It is Saturday. They are all in the country for two days – for an 'Activity Weekend'. Some of them don't really want to do the activity, but they all do it. ☐

b The people are from an office in the city. It is Saturday. They are all in the country for two days – for an 'Activity Weekend'. Some of them don't really want to do the activity and one person doesn't do it. ☐

c The people are from an office in the city. It is Saturday. They are all in the country for two days – for an 'Activity Weekend'. Everyone wants to do the activity but one person doesn't do it. ☐

Listen to Track 17. Were you right?

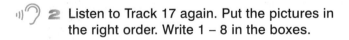

2 Listen to Track 17 again. Put the pictures in the right order. Write 1 – 8 in the boxes.

1 wall ☐
2 rope ladder ☐
3 tunnel ☐
4 tree house ☐
5 barbed wire ☐
6 plank ☐
7 wire ☐
8 mud ☐

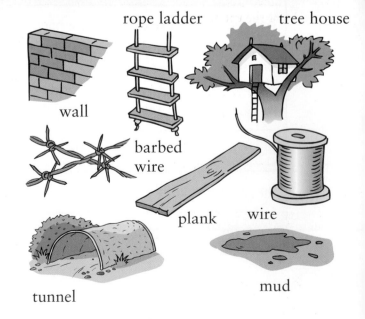

rope ladder   tree house

wall

barbed wire

plank   wire

tunnel   mud

3 Complete the instructions with the verbs in the box. You can use some verbs more than once. Listen to Track 17 again to help you, if necessary.

a .... towards the wall.

b .... up the wall.

c .... down the other side.

d .... through the tunnel.

e .... the rope ladder.

f .... along the wooden plank.

g .... from the wire.

h .... your way along the wire.

i .... into the mud.

j .... under the barbed wire.

| climb | crawl | drop | hang | jump | make | run | walk |

4 Look at the picture. Then complete the instructions.

First, (**a**) .... towards the barbed wire.

(**b**) .... under it.

Then (**c**) .... the plank to the other side of the mud.

(**d**) .... the wall.

Now (**e**) .... from the rope ladder and

(**f**) .... your way across it.

Finally, (**g**) .... off the end and try not to

(**h**) .... into the river.

Listen to Track 17 and check.

●● B Speaking

Interview

1 Choose one of the pictures and complete these tasks, using your imagination. Make notes.

What is the person's name?

....

....

How would this person describe himself / herself?

....

....

What does the person do?

....

....

What is the best thing about this job? And the worst?

....

....

Why did the person decide to do this job?

....

....

What are his / her future plans?

....

....

 2 Now imagine you are the person in the photo. Listen to Track 18 and answer the questions. Use your notes to help you.

A Listening

The soundtrack of our lives

1 **Listen to Track 19. Three friends are talking about songs. Who says these things, Sophie, Mandy or her boyfriend, Bill? Write the speaker's name.**

a 'Songs are like the soundtrack of our lives.' ....Sophie....

b 'I can remember the tune but I can't think of the name.'

....

c 'I bet you have a song that brings back memories.'

....

d 'I didn't know you liked romantic songs.' ....

e 'Every time I hear the song I can remember that summer as if it was yesterday. ....

f 'You sound like old people talking about old times!'

....

g 'You can't remember the song they were playing when we met?' ....

2 **Listen to Track 19 again. Complete the table.**

	Song	Reasons for liking the song
Sophie		
Mandy		
Bill		

3 Listen to Track 20. Some people are talking about important events in their lives. What question are they answering?

. . . .

4 Match the speakers and the photos.

5 Listen to Track 20 again. Which speaker says the following? What is each speaker referring to?

a I'd never seen anything so amazing before! Speaker .... , referring to ....

b I couldn't believe she didn't know. Speaker .... , referring to ....

c I felt so proud! Speaker .... , referring to ....

d I didn't think he would ever go out with me. Speaker .... , referring to ....

B Speaking
Memories

1 Put the pictures in order to tell a story. Name the boxes A – E. In your own words, record the story onto a tape.

2 Listen to what you have recorded and make a note of any corrections you want to make. Record the story again.

3 Now listen to Track 21. Someone else is telling the story. What are the similarities or differences between your stories?

••• A Listening
Radio phone-in

1 Look at the photos. Guess what the radio phone-in will be about.

tossing the caber

extreme ironing

canopying   car rallying

))) Now listen to Track 22 and see if you were right.

2 Answer these questions.

a How many people call the radio programme? ....

b What activities are mentioned in the radio programme? ....

))) **3** Listen to Track 22 again and answer the questions.

a What is Keith's hobby? ....

b What is the basic equipment for Extreme Ironing? ....

c What was Phil doing when he invented Extreme Ironing? ....

d What was Phil's favourite sport before Extreme Ironing? ....

e What kind of people do Extreme Ironing? ....

4 Listen to Track 22 again. Complete the advertisement using
information from the programme.

What is extreme ironing?

It's (a) .... , using an ordinary (b) ....
and (c) .... but instead of doing it in your living room
or kitchen, you do it in (d) .... places! For example, at
the top (e) .... , up a (f) .... or at
the bottom of the (g) .... !

Who does it?

People from different (h) .... – but you have to be a
little bit (i) .... !

Interested? Here's how to find out more about this fascinating sport!
Phone the (j) ....
.... !

5 Complete the chart
with information from
the radio phone-in and
personal information.
Listen to Track 22
again, if you need to.

	Extreme ironing	My favourite leisure activity
(a) Where can you practise it?		
(b) What do you need?		
(c) What kind of people do it?		

B Speaking

Role-play: giving information

You are the receptionist at an ice rink. Read the information in the leaflet.
Listen to Track 23 and answer the caller's questions.

Seibel Ice Rink offers a variety of classes, courses and open sessions for all abilities.

Family Session Sundays 10.00 - 11.30 am

Parents & Small Children school term time only - supervised play session - Monday 1.00 - 2.00 pm

Junior Ice Hockey For 8 - 16 years. Anyone welcome, turn up and play. Wednesdays 5.30 - 7.00 pm (8 - 11yrs) & Thursdays 8.15 - 10.15 pm (8 - 11yrs)

Beat On Ice an evening of skating in a lively nightclub atmosphere. Wednesdays 7.30 - 10.00 pm, Fridays 7.30 - 10.00 pm, Saturdays 10.30 am - 12.15 pm and 12.30 - 2.00 pm, Sundays 2.00 - 4.00 and 8.00 - 9.30 pm

After school sessions school term time only - Wednesday 2.00 - 5.30 pm, Friday 4.00 - 5.30 pm

Beginners' open session especially for those who don't like speed skaters whizzing past! Mondays 6.45 - 8.00 pm

Our ice-skating courses are for all ages and abilities. Each course runs for six weeks and the sessions consist of half an hour lesson and half an hour supervised practice time.

Maximum class size is 30

Anyone on a course gets free skate hire and entry to the Monday evening open sessions to do their practising!

Book through reception. Credit cards accepted.

A Listening

Scary story

1 Look at the pictures and put them in order to make a story. Think about these questions.

a What time is it? ....

b Why is Judy alone in the house?

....

c What is she doing?

....

d How is Judy probably feeling? How do you

know .... 🔑

2 Listen to Track 24 and check your answers. 🔑

3 Listen to Track 24 again. Write T (true) or F (false).

a That night Judy was looking after a baby. ☐

b The baby was in the room with Judy. ☐

c Judy was enjoying her evening. ☐

d The phone rang three times. ☐

e The first time the phone rang, Judy didn't worry. ☐

f The second time the phone rang, Judy was frightened. ☐

g The last time the phone rang, Judy knew it was John. ☐

h The baby was in his room. ☐ 🔑

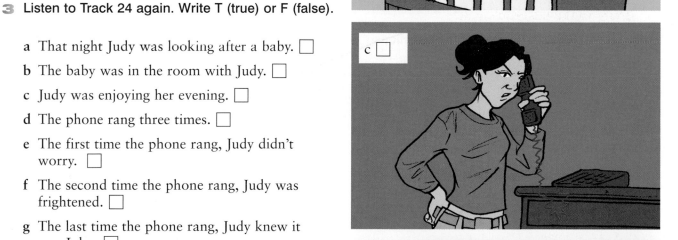

4 Now correct the sentences that are false.

....

....

....

.... 🔑

5 Without looking at the audioscript (or listening to Track 24 again), can you use the words in the box to reassemble a part of the dialogue? Use each word once only. Pay attention to capital letters, full stops (.), commas (,), question marks (?) and exclamation marks (!).

that	go	stop	empty
you	check	dropped	phone
John	on	stairs	up
is	the	looked	the
not	baby	cot	
funny	please	was	

JUDY: Is (a) .... This (b) .... so (c) ....

MAN: Go (d) .... baby.

JUDY: (e) .... this.

MAN: (f) .... check on the baby.

NARRATOR: Judy (g) .... the (h) .... and ran (i) ....

She (j) .... into the (k) ....'s (l) ....

The baby's cot (m) ....

Check your answers by listening to Track 24 again, and reading the audioscript on page 72.

. . . .

6 Listen to Track 25. Answer the questions.

a Where was Timmy, the baby? ....

b Who was the man on the phone? ....

c What does Judy think about it all? ....

•B Speaking
A newspaper report

1 Look at the picture and complete these tasks, using your imagination. Make notes.

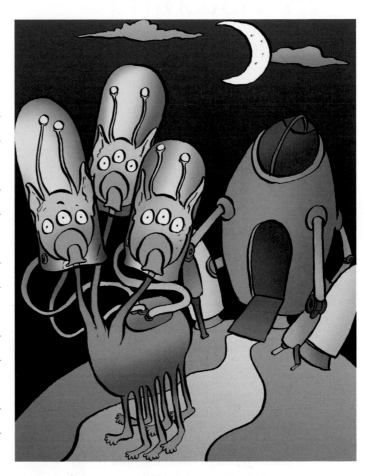

When did you see this?

....

....

Can you describe in detail what you saw?

....

....

What do you think it was?

....

....

How did you feel?

....

....

What did you do?

....

....

What happened in the end?

....

....

2 A newspaper reporter is interviewing you about what you saw. Listen to Track 26 and answer the questions. Use your notes to help you.

A Listening
Phone messages

1 **Listen to Track 27. Tick the correct picture for each of the messages.**

message 1

a ☐

b ☐

c ☐

message 2

d ☐

message 3

2 **Listen to Track 27 again. Who can you see in the pictures? Write Debbie, Peter, Melanie, Lucy, Will, Olga or Libby for each message (Warning: you can not see all of them!)**

Message 1 ....

Message 2 ....

Message 3 ....

e ☐

f ☐

3 **Answer the questions.**

a Who has a laptop? ....

b Who left something at home? ....

c Who apologises? ....

d Who is going to be late? ....

e Who's going to buy sandwiches? ....

f Who's having a party? ....

4 Put the words in the right order to make message announcements.

a at / call / can't / moment / take / the / We / your

....

b a / after / leave / message / Please / the / tone

....

c can't / come / I / now / phone / right / the / to

....

d you / a / and / back / I'll / Leave / message / ring

....

5 Listen to Track 28 and find the matching message.

A

John, urgent problem next door. Millie's there. Please feed her at 7. Food in sink.

B

John, urgent problem at office. Back at about 7. Millie next door, please fetch and feed her. Food in cupboard under sink.

C

John, urgent problem at office next door. Back at about 7. Please fetch Millie and feed her, in cupboard under sink.

Answer: ....

6 Now choose the other two messages in exercise 5. Practise leaving the messages on an answerphone. Listen to Track 29 and compare.

B Speaking
Describing objects

1 Match the words and the pictures.

mobile phone   video games console   camcorder   MP3 player
computer   radio   digital camera   three-wheeled motorbike

a ....

b ....

c ....

d ....

e ....

f ....

g ....

h ....

2 Listen to Track 30. Which four objects in the pictures are the people describing?

....

....

....

....

3 Choose one of the objects in the picture. Complete the dialogue about it. Then listen to Track 31 and speak when it is your turn.

Tell me about the object you have chosen. But don't say what it's called! How big is it?

....

What colour is it?

....

What do you use it for, or do with it?

....

Do you have one of these yourself?

....

How often do you use it?

....

Now say what you have been describing.

....

A Listening

Clayton Street

1 Listen to the scene from the soap opera Clayton Street on Track 32. Look at the pictures. Write Jezza or Chris under the correct picture.

2 Listen to Track 32 again. Circle the best answer.

a Jezza
   1 is a good friend to Chris.
   2 is not a good friend to Chris.
b Chris
   1 is unhappy because Jezza didn't put his number in the 'phonebook' on his mobile phone.
   2 is not happy because Jezza didn't remember his number.
c Chris
   1 wants his money back.
   2 is going to give Jezza some money.
d Chris
   1 is sure that he will get £200 from Jezza.
   2 isn't sure that he will get £200 from Jezza.
e Jezza
   1 will give Chris £200 tomorrow.
   2 won't give Chris £200 tomorrow.

a ....

b ....

3 Look at the lines from Track 32. Look at the verbs in the box. Complete them with the correct form of the verbs in the box.

a Where it .... you the numbers?

b You .... me in your phonebook, haven't you?

c I don't .... it.

d But what do you .... ?

e I .... you two hundred pounds, remember.

f I'll .... it to you tomorrow.

g You .... that before.

h You'll .... your money tomorrow.

i I .... go.

| believe   have got |
| have got to   get   give |
| lend   say   show   want |

Listen to Track 32 again. Were you correct?

4 Look at the pictures and guess the answers to these questions.

a Do you think this episode of Clayton Street comes after the one
   on page 33, or before? Why? ....

b Why doesn't Jezza want an office job? ....

c What is Chris' job? ....

d What is Jezza's dream job? ....

e Why does Jezza want Chis' money? ....

Now listen to Track 33 and check your answer.

5 Listen to Track 33 again and write T (true) or F (false) in the boxes.

a Jezza doesn't mind being unemployed. ☐

b Chris hasn't got a boring office job. ☐

c Jezza hasn't ever done any DJ-ing. ☐

d Jezza believes friends should lend each other money. ☐

e Jezza is confident that he will be able to pay Chris back. ☐

B Speaking
The best present

1 Listen to Track 34 and choose the correct picture (a – d) below.

a

b

c

d

....

2 Answer the questions about <u>your</u> best present.

Who gave it to you?

....

When did you get it?

....

Do you still have it?

....

Why is / was it special to you?

....

....

3 Now listen to Track 35 and speak when it is your turn.

•• A Listening

A scene from a play

1 Listen to Track 36 and put the sound effects in the right order. The first one is done for you.

a a knock at the door

b the sound of a mobile phone

c the sound of drinking

d the window crashes open

e someone closes the window

f the sound of change / coins

g the sound of stirring with a spoon

h the sound of the door handle

i thunder

2 Charles and Miranda pull a bed across the floor. Do they do this before or after (h)? ....

3 Listen to Track 36 again. Who says the following? Write *the man* or *the woman*.

a It's a bit dark. ....the man........

b Don't worry, dear. ....

c I loved it. ....

d I'm not very strong. ....

e It's scary. ....

f Nonsense! ....

g Nothing to worry about. ....

h Come on. Help me. ....

i That's better. ....

j We're safe now. ....

4   What do we know about:

  a the type of hotel? ....

  b the man's and the woman's characters? ....

  c what the man and woman like to drink? ....

  d the name of the hotel? .... 🔑

5   Listen to Track 36 again and complete the following questions from the conversation.

  a It's scary, ... ?

  b That's better, ... ?

  c We're safe, ... ?

  d You didn't put it in your bag, ... ?

  e It's not in my bag, ... ? 🔑

6   Make the sentences into questions like the questions in exercise 5.

  a This is a nice hotel, ... ?

  b The water's very cold, ... ?

  c They stayed here last year, ... ?

  d She likes chocolate, ... ?

  e This isn't a very good painting, ... ?

  f The water isn't very warm, ... ?

  g She didn't leave her bag in the restaurant, ... ?

  h They aren't going to be late, ... ? 🔑

  What is the difference between sentences a – d and sentences e – h? 🔑

7   Answer the questions.

  a What did Miranda think of the hotel room? ....

  b What did the waiter bring Charles? And Miranda? ....

  c What kind of holiday did they go on before? ....

  d What did Miranda think of it? ....

  e Where was Miranda's phone? ....

  f Who was phoning her? ....

  g Why? ....

  Listen to Track 36 again to check. 🔑

●●B Speaking

Ambitions

I want to visit
New York.

Before I'm thirty? I want
to climb Mount Everest.

I would like to
learn how to fly.

I want to have
at least six
children.

I would like to
play football for
my country.

I want to
write a novel.

I would like to have
my own business.

1 Complete the sentences in your own words.

Before I'm thirty / forty / fifty I want to have ....

....

I want to ....

....

I would like to ....

....

I would like to learn ....

....

I want to visit ....

....

I'm going to ....

....

I intend to ....

....

2 Record your sentences onto a tape. Listen and make notes of any corrections you want to make. Record your sentences again.

A Listening

Radio advertisements

1 Listen to Track 37. Match the advertisements with the pictures. Write 1 – 5 in the boxes. 🔑

2 Listen to Track 37 again. Are these statements true or false? Write T or F in the boxes.

a The Fire Service only fights fires. ☐

b You can get 20% off when you buy something in the Kenneth Cole store. ☐

c Battersea Dogs Home has dogs and cats. ☐

d Friends of the Earth just protects wild animals. ☐

e You can learn to be a clown at a school. ☐ 🔑

3 Listen to Track 37 again and complete these statements with the words you hear.

a When we get a call it could be to a road accident, an air accident or a rail accident or to .... someone from a lift.

b The shoes and clothes that you give us, we'll give to the ....

c They are here at the Battersea Dogs and Cats Home because their .... left them in the street to die.

d We are looking for .... to help us with sending out letters and making telephone calls.

e Come to the California .... School where you will learn the art of clowning. 🔑

a ☐

b ☐

c ☐

d ☐

e ☐

4   Listen to Track 37 again and complete these written ads.

Kenneth Cole Stores are helping (a) ....

Special offer until (b) ....

Bring in your old (c) .... and
(d) .... and we'll give you
(e) .... off the next thing you buy in our store!

Can you give (f) ....
.... and (g) .... a home?
Here at Battersea (h) ....
we rescue dogs and (i) .... and
(j) .... new homes for them. Visit our
website at (k) .... for more
information.

Have you got any free time? (l) .... of the
(m) .... needs volunteers to help with
(n) .... and (o) ....
Give us a ring on Freephone (p) ....

•• B Speaking

Meeting: Who shall we invite?

1   You are at a meeting to decide on a person to invite to come and speak to your English class. You would like to invite Emily Davis. Read about her.

Making a difference:

Working with homeless children

Name:	Emily Davis
Comes from:	California
Reason she joined volunteer project with children in Ecuador:	Always wanted to work with children, and help with social work and teaching. Interested in Ecuador because of degree in Spanish / Latin American studies at university.
Work she did there:	Everything, from teaching English, correcting Spanish and other homework, to group activities, guitar lessons, sports lessons.
Difficulties:	Sometimes controlling the kids was a bit difficult – they had lots of energy!
Contribution to the community:	Children learnt that there are lots of opportunities for them. Many went on to study further, and help their own community in turn.

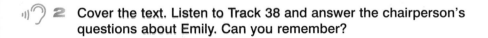

2   Cover the text. Listen to Track 38 and answer the chairperson's questions about Emily. Can you remember?

A Listening

Remembering schooldays

1 Listen to Brian and Molly on Track 39. Which teacher did …

 a Molly like best, Mrs Gladwin or Ms Marley? ....

 b Brian like best, Mrs Gladwin or Ms Marley? ....

2 Which teachers (or their classes) do these sentences describe? Write G (Mrs Gladwin) or
M (Ms Marley) in the boxes.

 a 'She used to say, 'Don't do this, don't do that!' all the time. ☐

 b We sat in rows for hours. ☐

 c We were afraid to talk. ☐

 d Sometimes we played all day. ☐

 e I'm not sure I learned anything with her. ☐

 f We learned by ourselves. ☐

 g She was always so grumpy. ☐

 h She was lovely. ☐

3 Listen to Track 39 again. Read the opinions a – f. Which teacher has each opinion?
Write G or M in the boxes.

 a Children need discipline. ☐

 b Children can stop and start activities when they want. ☐

 c Children can discover things for themselves. ☐

 d Children of different ages can all work together. ☐

 e Children of different ages should be separate. ☐

 f Children need to be happy and comfortable. ☐

4 Choose a word from the box to complete each part of the conversations on Track 39.

 a Remember how she was so .... with us? 'Do this, don't do that' all the time.

 b We were all really quiet – afraid to talk. She was really one for .... , huh?

 c Ms Marley? Oh yeah – she was great – young and ....

 d I was always talking with my friends – the whole class went .... sometimes.

 e She never really told us anything. We learned by ....

 f Mrs Gladwin used to put us in separate groups so the big kids didn't .... the little kids.

 g You know, I think the most important thing is personal ....

frighten	strict
friendly	ourselves
wild	attention
discipline	

5 Adam and Jessica were at secondary school together five years ago. They are remembering some of their old school friends. Listen to Track 40. Match the names with the photos.

Anne ☐

Luke ☐

Pablo ☐

Elsa ☐ 🔑

6 Listen to Track 40 again and answer the questions.

a What was Anne like?

....

b What did she use to do when teachers spoke to her?

....

c What was Elsa's talent?

....

d Who did she use to go out with?

....

e What did he look like?

....

f What annoying thing did Luke use to do in class?

....

g What did he look like?

....

h Did Jessica like him? How do you know?

....

•• B Speaking
The education debate

1 Why do we need to go to school? Match each reason with one of the pictures. Write a – h in the boxes.

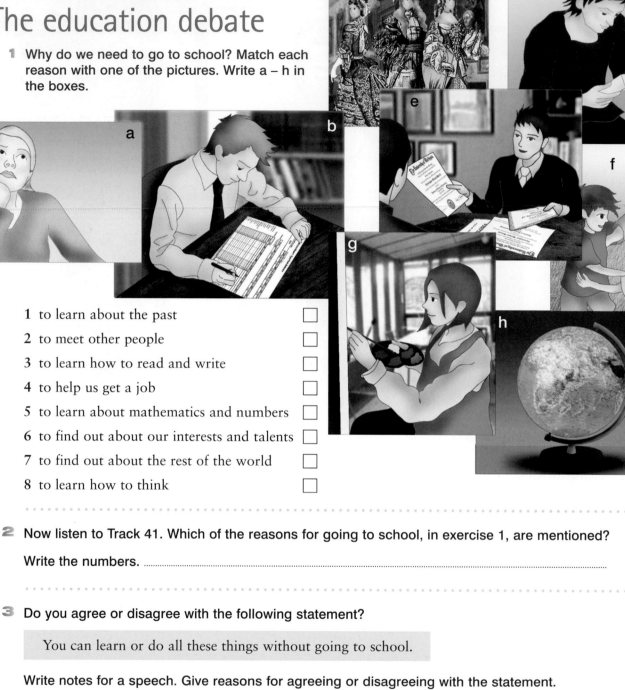

1 to learn about the past ☐

2 to meet other people ☐

3 to learn how to read and write ☐

4 to help us get a job ☐

5 to learn about mathematics and numbers ☐

6 to find out about our interests and talents ☐

7 to find out about the rest of the world ☐

8 to learn how to think ☐

2 Now listen to Track 41. Which of the reasons for going to school, in exercise 1, are mentioned?

Write the numbers. ....

3 Do you agree or disagree with the following statement?

> You can learn or do all these things without going to school.

Write notes for a speech. Give reasons for agreeing or disagreeing with the statement.

....

....

....

....

....

4 Record your speech. Listen to your speech, and make any corrections. Record yourself again.

•• **A** Listening

The news

🔊 **1** Listen to Track 42. Tick the people and things that you hear.

a airport ☐   h Queen ☐

b car crash ☐   i rivers ☐

c dog ☐   j storms ☐

d egg ☐   k student ☐

e mountains ☐   l the environment ☐

f nurses ☐   m tower ☐

g Prime Minister ☐

2 Match the people and the items from exercise 1. The first one is done for you.

a Antonia Merritt .... *car crash* ....

b Mark Gartside ....

c Phyllis Jones ....

d Stephen Williams ....

3 Who or what ...?

a barked and barked? ....

b designed a new building? ....

c doesn't have a job? ....

d fell in her house? ....

e is going to be an Egyptian queen in a new film? ....

f likes architects? ....

g talked to the police? ....

h thanked doctors? ....

i thanked her dog? ....

j visited a new building? ....

k was at a press conference? ....

l won a prize? ....

4   Complete three of the newspaper articles with the missing words. Then listen
     to Track 42 again and check.

Prime Minister attacked

A (a) .... -year-old man, Stephen Williams, threw (b) .... at the
Prime Minister today as he was arriving at the New London Tower. Williams
told the police he was (c) .... about the (d) ....
The Prime Minister was not hurt, and (e) .... about the incident.

Student wins prize

A (f) .... -year-old student, Mike Gartside, has won the
National (g) .... prize for his design for a new
London (h) .... on the (i) .... It is
Mr Gartside's first full design.

Dog saves owner

Phyllis Jones, aged (j) .... , fell in her house and
couldn't get off the (k) .... The dog barked and
barked until someone (l) .... him and came to
see what the (m) .... was. 'My dog gave me my
(n) .... back,' said Mrs Jones.

B Speaking
What is it like?

1 Look at the photos. Can you name the buildings?

a The Deep, in Hull, England – an 'underwater exhibition' centre ☐

b Selfridges Department store in Birmingham, England ☐

c The Modern Art Centre, Cincinnatti, USA ☐

d The opera house in Santa Cruz, Tenerife (Canary Islands) ☐

. . . .

2 Read this description. Which building does it describe?

> It's a modern building. I don't like it very much, because it looks rather ugly. It looks like a monster's face, with one eye and a mouth. ☐

. . . .

3 Now write notes describing the three other buildings. Listen to Track 43 and answer the questions.

Useful phrases

It looks like a ... (+ noun)
It looks ... (+ adjective)

Useful adjectives

big   cold   dramatic   exciting   friendly
modern   tall   ugly   unfinished

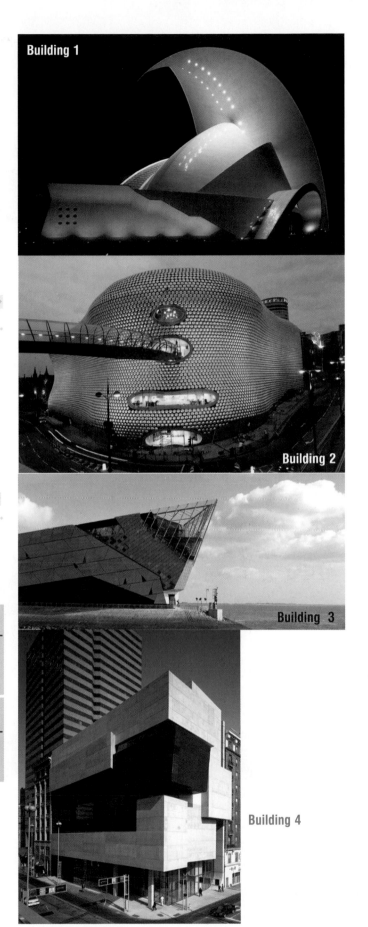

Building 1

Building 2

Building 3

Building 4

•• A Listening

It's all in the eyes

1 Look at this photo of the eyes. What do you think this person is thinking?

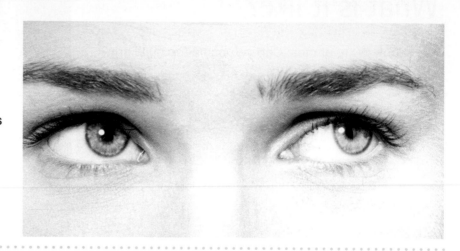

2 Match the sentences with the pictures. Write a – f in the boxes.

a she is looking down and to the left

b she is looking directly left

c she is looking up and to the left

d she is looking directly right

e she is looking up and to the right

f she is looking down and to the right

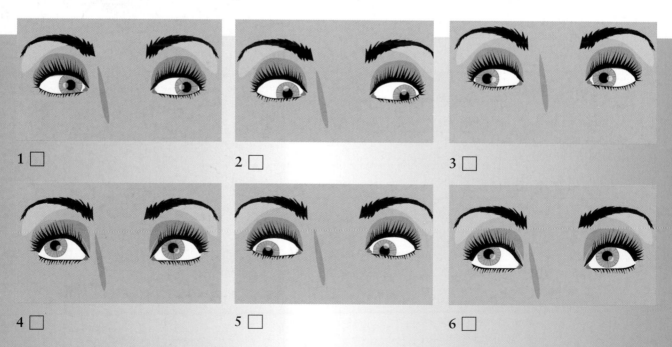

1 ☐   2 ☐   3 ☐

4 ☐   5 ☐   6 ☐

3 Listen to Track 44 and answer write T (Tricia) of M (Marty) for the sentences.

Who...

a tries to remember the face of a childhood friend? ☐

b read an article about brain research and eye movement? ☐

c says people's eyes move in different directions when they think about different things? ☐

d can't stop looking into people's eyes? ☐

4 Listen to Track 44 again. Match the eye position from exercise 2 for the activities.
Write 1 – 6 in the boxes. The first one is done for you.

a remembering an image   1

b inventing an image   ☐

c remembering a sound   ☐

d imagining a sound   ☐

e talking to yourself   ☐

f having feelings   ☐

5 According to Marty's article, which way does it say you will look when you think about:

a a time when you felt scared?..

b the sound of a big dog barking? ....

c the sound of your mother's voice? ....

d the face of a person you know? ....

e a picture of a high mountain? ....

f how you are going to solve a problem? ....

Listen to Track 44 again to check.

•••B Speaking
Your health

1 Answer the questions in the questionnaire.

Sleep

1 How much sleep do you get every night?

....

2 What time do you usually go to bed?

....

3 How do you usually feel when you wake up?

....

4 Do you fall asleep easily, or do you have trouble falling asleep?

....

5 Do you ever wake up in the night? Why?

....

6 What is the last thing you usually do before going to sleep?

....

Diet

7 What do you have for breakfast?

....

8 What do you usually have for lunch?

....

9 What did you have for dinner last night? Is this typical?

....

10 How much water do you drink every day?

....

11 Do you think your diet needs to improve? In what way?

....

Fitness

12 How much physical activity do you do every day?

....

....

13 Would you like to get fitter? How?

....

....

14 What new sport would you like to take up, if you could?

....

....

2 Now listen to Track 45 and answer the questions.

Listening
Unidentified Flying Objects

1 Look at these two photos. What do they show? Do you believe the photographs are real?

2 You are going to listen to two stories about UFOs. Read these sentences about each story, and put them in the correct order. Then listen to Track 46 and check your answers.

A

B

a It was moving at 600 mph. ☐
b He gave the photos to experts to study. ☐
c One of them took photos of it. ☐
d People living on an island began to see strange things in the sky. ☐
e These included discs that were flying fast. ☐
f Then one night, 47 people, on a ship in the area, saw a strange disc. ☐

a They took lights, a radio and a Geiger counter to measure radiation. ☐
b Security guards saw unusual lights in the forest. ☐
c The next day there were broken trees and holes in the ground. ☐
d This happened for two nights. ☐
e The lights and radio stopped working, and the Geiger counter started to make noises. ☐
f On the second night, they went into the forest to investigate. ☐

3 Listen to Track 46 again. Write 1, 2 or 3 to answer each question for each story.

	A	B
a Where did the story take place? 1 Trindade Islands, Brazil 2 Harvard University, USA 3 Bentwaters, England		
b When did the story take place? 1 December 1st 1957 2 December 27th 1980 3 January 16th 1958		
c What did people see first? 1 unusual lights 2 discs flying very fast 3 slow discs and lights		
d How big was the object that people saw? 1 20 feet wide and 30 feet high 2 47 feet high 3 50 feet wide		
e Were there any photographs or other physical evidence? 1 a noisy aeroplane 2 a series of six photographs 3 broken trees and large holes in the ground		
f What was the explanation given by people who did not believe the story? 1 it was an aeroplane flying through the fog 2 it was the wind and complex scientific causes 3 it was a radio station		
g What do people say today? 1 the objects moved slowly 2 the photographs are real 3 experts cannot explain the high levels of radiation		

B Speaking
Phone call

1 **1 Read the text and answer the questions.**

a Why did Andy used to hate to be alone when he was a child? ....

b Who was the man who called him in 1985?

....

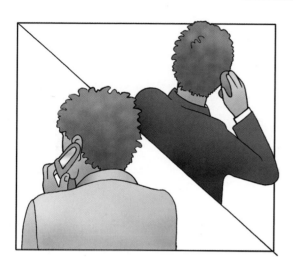

All his life, Andy Jackson hated to be alone. As a child, he always wanted someone to stay the night at his house. As a young man, he had several different friends. He always felt that he was not complete – there was something missing from his life.

That ended on Sept. 23, 1985, when the telephone rang and a voice said, "You don't know me, and this is a strange question, but when were you born?" Andy thought it was odd, but gave the answer. "Well, here's an even stranger question for you: Were you adopted?" Andy said "yes". "Hi," the stranger said. "I'm your twin brother."

Andy did not know that he had a brother. When they were born they were given to two different couples. Andy discovered that his brother's name was Kevin and soon found that there were many similarities and differences between them.

 2 **Read the notes about Andy. Listen to Track 47 and speak when it is Andy's part.**

Andy
Occupation: manager of a supermarket
Family: Married for ten years to Jane (cashier), three children (Brad, 8, Molly, 4, Johnny, 3)
Education: didn't go to university, left school at 18
Personality: calm, relaxed
Home: large house about 70 km from Los Angeles, California

3 **Read the notes about Kevin. Listen to Track 47 again and speak when it is Kevin's part.**

Kevin
Occupation: manager of a bookstore
Family: Married for three years to Mary (police officer), three children (Brad, 6 months, twins Kevin and Susie, 2)
Education: studied English at college
Personality: serious, ambitious
Home: large apartment in Los Angeles, California

4 **Now write down the similarities between Andy and Kevin.**

....
....
....
....
....
....
....
....
....
....
....
....
....

●● A: Sounds

1 Listen to Track 48. Number the words in the order of the track. Write 1 – 8 in the boxes.

a television [1]   e decision ☐
b usual ☐   f obsession ☐
c information ☐   g solution ☐
d fashion ☐   h conclusion ☐

2 Listen to Track 48 again. Write the words in the table.

Words with the sound /ʒ/ like *pleasure*	Words with the sounds /ʃ/ like *ship*

Listen to Track 48 again and repeat the words.

3 The words in *italics* in the dialogues below have the sounds /ʃ/ or /ʒ/ in them. Write the words in *italics* under the correct sound.

/ʃ/	/ʒ/
sugar	

a A: How do you like your tea?
   B: With *sugar, usually*.
b A: Come on then. What's the solution?
   B: There is no *solution*. That's my *conclusion*.
c A: What are you doing?
   B: Watching a *fashion* show on *television*.
d A: So, what do you think?
   B: We can make a *decision* after our *discussion*.

Listen to Track 49. Check your answers. Then listen again and repeat the words.

4 Listen to Track 50. Read the answers in the dialogues in exercise 3 when it's your turn.

5 Listen to Track 51. Complete the table with the words in the box. Look at the underlined sound in two- or three-syllable words.

Amelie   back   clock   drop   front   hang   jump   ladder   mud   opposite   plank   platform   scanned   someone   son   top   tunnel   under

/ɒ/ - cop	/æ/ - cap	/ʌ/ - cup
	Amelie	

Play Track 50 again. Say the words after the speakers.

6 Listen to Track 52 and write /e/ or /ei/ according to the vowel sound you hear.

a   /e/   check
b
c
d
e
f

g
h
i
j
k

Now listen again and write the word on the line.

Practise saying the words with the correct pronunciation.

7 Listen to Track 53. Number the words in the order of the track. Write 1 – 12 in the boxes.

a sin   ☐   e ran   ☐   i sinner   ☐
b sing   ☐1   f rang   ☐   j singer   ☐
c tonne ☐   g sun   ☐   k thin   ☐
d tongue ☐   h sung   ☐   l thing   ☐

Write the words with the sound /n/ like *none*?

....

Write the words with the sound /ŋ/ like *long*?

....

8 Listen to Track 54. Number the words in the order you hear them.

bingo   ☐1   sung   ☐
drink   ☐   swimming   ☐
fun   ☐   thin   ☐
no   ☐   thing   ☐
sound   ☐   think   ☐
sun   ☐   thanks   ☐

C: Intonation

1 Listen to Track 85. Does the speaker's voice go up, or down? Write *up* or *down* in the blanks.

    a Do you like your job? ....

    b Do you enjoy it? ....

    c Is it dangerous? ....

    d Do you have a good job? ....

    e Is the money good? ....

Listen to Track 85 again and repeat the questions.

2 Listen to Track 86. Does the speaker's voice go up or down?

    a Are you looking for a job? ....*up*...........

    b Are you interested in people? ....

    c Are you good with animals? ....

    d Can you work in a team? ....

    e Do you like working with animals? ....

Listen again and repeat the questions.

3 Listen to this radio advertisement in Track 87. Does the speaker say the questions with the same intonation as in exercise 2 above? Underline the question where the intonation is different.

Then practise reading the advert aloud.

4 Listen to these exclamations on Track 88. Are the speakers interested (and / or amused) or bored (and / or disapproving)? Write I (interested or amused) or B (bored or disapproving) in the boxes.

    a How funny! ☐

    b How stupid! ☐

    c How silly! ☐

    d How boring! ☐

    e How lovely! ☐

Are you looking for a job?

How would you like to help animals?

Can you work in a team?

Yes?

We've got the perfect job for you!

Call the Animal Hospital **NOW!**

No experience required!

5 Listen to Track 89 and repeat these exclamations with the correct intonation.

    a How nice!
    b How awful!
    c How funny!
    d How boring!
    e How exciting!

6 Listen to Track 90. After the beep, use an exclamation from exercise 5 above to react to what the speakers say.

    a I have to work on Saturday.
       YOU: .... *How boring!* ....

    b My grandfather fell and broke his leg.
       YOU: .... !

    c I'm going to Australia!
       YOU: .... !

    d Ryan got married in a Superman suit!
       YOU: .... !

    e Look, I bought you an ice cream.
       YOU: .... !

7 Look at the groups of questions. Why are they different?

    a What's her number? ....
       How can I help? ....
       Who's calling, please? ....
    b Is Rose there? ....
       Do you have his number? ....
       Can I help you? ....

8 Listen to Track 91. Does the voice go up or down? Mark ⌒↘ (down) or ↘⌝ (up) in the blanks.

Which questions (a or b above) go up? Which go down?

↘⌝ ....

⌒↘ ....

one day he asked me if I wanted to go and have a Coke with him after school. That was our first date! I remember going home afterwards, thinking, I've got a boyfriend! But sadly, that was it. We didn't have another date, ever.

I wonder what he's doing now …

Track 21

Linda and her best friend Joe grew up together. They used to play together as children. They were best friends until they left school. Then Linda went to college in another state. Joe became an engineer in another country. She and Joe didn't see each other often after that. Many years passed, and Linda became a nurse in a big hospital. One of her patients was an old man, who she really liked a lot. When it was time for him to go home, she knew she would miss him. He reminded her of someone, but she couldn't think who it was …. The old man told Linda his grandson was coming to pick him up and take him home. He told her a lot about his grandson. Linda thought he sounded very kind, to look after his grandfather so well. She went to meet him. It was Joe! Imagine their surprise, when they realised they had found each other again after all this time! The story has a happy ending. Joe and Linda got married, and Joe's grandparents were there to celebrate with them.

Track 22

DJ: Welcome back to 'Talktime', the morning show for you, the listeners. Today's topic is leisure. What do you do in your spare time – when you're not working or studying? Do you do anything unusual? Anything wacky? Give us a call. And we have a caller on the line. It's Keith. Hello, Keith. What do you like doing?

KEITH: Hi Jim! My hobby is Extreme Ironing.

DJ: Wait a minute, what did you say? Extreme Ironing?

KEITH: Yeah, that's right. Ironing. You know, with an iron and an ironing board.

DJ: Sorry, Keith, but do you mean ironing, the kind I do – like ironing clothes?

KEITH: Well, yeah, but, with a difference. In Extreme Ironing you don't do the ironing in the kitchen or the bedroom. You do it in strange, unusual places.

DJ: Like what?

KEITH: Well, like at the top of a mountain, or up a tree, or at the bottom of the sea … Anywhere! It's up to you and your imagination!

DJ: Are you serious?

KEITH: Of course I am.

DJ: But that's just …, it's just …

KEITH: Just crazy! Yes it is, it's great fun and you need a lot of skill.

DJ: Er … yeah. Hey Keith, do other people do this Extreme Ironing or is it just you?

KEITH: No, no! It's not just me. People do Extreme Ironing all over the world. We even have World Championships.

DJ: Wow! Fantastic. So how did this … um … sport start?

KEITH: Well it all started with a guy called Phil. He was

doing his ironing and he was bored. He started to think about his favourite sport.

DJ: His favourite sport?

KEITH: Yeah. Phil loves rock climbing, and he thought 'rock climbing … ironing … ironing … rock climbing' and that was it!

DJ: Who does Extreme Ironing then?

KEITH: Lots of people from lots of different countries. You have to enjoy life and be a bit crazy!

DJ: So if any listeners are interested, how can they find out more about it?

KEITH: You can find us on the Internet or phone the Extreme Ironing Offices. They're in the phone book.

DJ: You heard it here first! That was Keith the ironing man! Our next caller is Sue. Hello. Sue, what's your favourite activity?

SUE: Hello Jim! My favourite activity is canopying, like in the jungle. You know, flying through the tops of trees? I did this in Costa Rica last summer and it's really awesome …

Track 23

Hello, I'm interested in ice skating at your ice rink. Can you tell me what time the beginner sessions are? I'm not very good, so I don't want to skate too fast.

And what about family sessions? What days do you run these?

What time do they start and finish?

Right. And what about courses? Do you have courses for family groups, or are they only for children?

How long do the courses last?

How many students in a class?

What's included in the price?

Where can I book?

Can I pay by credit card?

OK, thanks! It sounds fun. I'll come in and make a booking tomorrow.

Track 24

MAN: Radio Triple X presents 'Turn out the Light – and Listen'.

NARRATOR: It all happened on a quiet summer's night. 19-year-old Judy was babysitting for the Donovan family. When she got to the house Mrs Donovan said 'the baby's already asleep, Judy, so you can just watch TV, OK?'. That was enough for Judy. She turned on the television and started to watch an old romantic film.

JUDY: Oh no! Just when the film is getting exciting! Hello?
Hello? Hmm, probably the wrong number.

JUDY: Not again! Who can it be at this time of night? Hello? Who is this? Hello?
Oh well, suit yourself.

NARRATOR: Judy was a bit worried. But then she smiled. Her boyfriend, John was probably playing a joke.

JUDY: Is that you John? This is so not funny!

MAN: Go check on the baby.

JUDY: Please stop this.

MAN: Go check on the baby.

NARRATOR: Judy dropped the phone and ran up the stairs. She looked into the baby's cot. The baby's cot was empty!

Track 25

JUDY: Hello?

WOMAN: Hello? Judy? Finally! My phone wasn't working. Listen, I forgot to tell you. Timmy isn't in his cot tonight. He's in our bed. Can you just check on him?

JUDY: All right, Mrs Donovan, but a man keeps calling –

WOMAN: No, not again. That's my crazy brother. He does that sometimes. But don't worry, dear. It's just his idea of a joke.

JUDY: Ha ha.

Track 26

When exactly did you see this?

Can you describe in detail what you saw?

What did it look like?

What was it doing?

What do you think it was?

Did it say or do anything to you?

How did you feel?

What did you do?

What happened in the end?

Thank you very much, it's certainly a very scary story. Now, if anyone else has seen anything like this, could they please call the station on ….

Track 27

1

MESSAGE: This is 758967356. We can't take your call at the moment. Please leave a message after the tone.

MALE CALLER: Erm, Debbie, this is Peter. I'm sorry but I can't meet you at 12. How about a bit later, around 2? We can meet outside the library. Oh, and can you bring your laptop with you? And don't forget the library books. We have to return them today. See you later!

2

GIRL 1: Hiya! I can't come to the phone right now – leave a message and I'll ring you back.

GIRL 2: Melanie? It's Lucy. Listen, I left the tickets on the kitchen table! Bring them with you! And can you get some sandwiches for the train? See you outside the station at 12, under the clock. Don't be late!

3

FEMALE VOICE 1: This is Olga

FEMALE VOICE 2: and Libby!

OLGA: We're not here right now. Leave a message

LIBBY: and we'll call you back!

MALE CALLER: Hi! It's Will. Listen, we have a big problem for the party tonight – my sound system is broken! Can you bring yours? Is that all right? And bring some dance music. Oh, and something to eat? Crisps or something? Thanks. See you!

Track 28

John, it's me. Listen, there's been an urgent problem …. I had to come into the office for a couple of hours. Anyway I've taken Millie next door. But can you fetch her and feed her? She'll be really hungry. And I won't be back before 7. Oh, you'll find her food under the sink, you know, in the cupboard there. I've written you a note about it too – it's on the fridge. See you later, OK? Bye!

Track 29

A

John, it's me. Listen there's been an urgent problem next door. Millie's there. Can you please feed her at 7? Her food's in the sink. OK? Bye!

C

John, it's me. Listen, there's been an urgent problem at the office next door. I'll be back at about 7. Please fetch Millie and feed her in the cupboard under the sink. OK? Bye!

Track 30

1

A: Do you think we should bring the (beep) with us this evening?

B: Yes, that's a great idea. We can take photos of us all together. Then when we get home, we can email them to everyone. That'll be a good way to remember this occasion, don't you think?

2

Hello, Mum, it's me, I just had an idea. Since you and Dad can't come to little Jessie's school concert, maybe I could borrow your (beep) and film it? That way we can all watch it together afterwards at your place.

3

Hello, this is Paul Barrett. I'm not in the office right now, but you can reach me on my (beep), so please call me if you need me. The number is 089850…

4

A: Hello, Sam! Happy birthday!

B: Thanks! Guess what my parents got me. A (beep)!

A: Oh, wow!

B: And two games for it! Do you want to come round and play?

Track 31

Tell me about the object you have chosen. But don't say what it's called! How big is it?

What colour is it?

What do you use it for, or do with it?

Do you have one of these yourself?

How often do you use it?

Now say what you have been describing.

Track 69

a   sun glasses
b   guide book
c   subway station
d   cash dispenser
e   ski resort
f   hotel room
g   police station

Track 70

a   phone box
b   letter box
c   tea cup
d   road signs
e   park bench
f   traffic lights
g   cricket match
h   underground station

Track 71

boring, tired, people
advice, excuse, repeat

Track 72

a   explain
b   healthy
c   accept
d   diet
e   massage
f   lifestyle
g   problem
h   complete

Track 73

a   problem, problem
b   result, result

Track 74

c   coffee
d   chocolate
e   water
f   inside
g   salad
h   without
i   practise

Track 75

a
Can you remember him?
Yes, I can. I can remember him clearly.
b
He was tall.
And handsome!
Yes, he was tall and handsome.
c
Was he there?
Yes, he was.
What was he doing?
He was dancing.

Track 76

a
MAN: Was the test difficult?
GIRL: No. It was nice and easy.
b
WOMAN: Can you come and help?
MAN: Yes, I can. But I can only stay for an hour.
c
WOMAN: How was your holiday?
MAN: Jamaica was hot and humid!
WOMAN: But was it nice?
MAN: Oh, it was beautiful – and a lot of fun!

Track 77

a   Was the test difficult?
BEEP
b   Can you come and help?
BEEP
c   How was your holiday?
BEEP
d   But was it nice?
BEEP

Track 78

Are you going to come to the party with us?
Are you gonna come to the party with us?

Track 79

a   What are you going to do when you leave school?
b   I think I'm gonna stay at home tonight. I'm tired.
c   Well, first I'm going to get my doctorate, then I'm going to live in South America.
d   She's not gonna be there, I'm afraid. She's gonna be in the library.

Track 80

a   We're gonna go to the beach.
b   She's going to win.
c   James is going to study French.
d   They're gonna tell you to stop.

Track 81

beautiful
ugly
delicious
horrible
enjoyable
boring
frightening
bad
cheap
cramped
deep
expensive
fast
fat
funny
good
high

interesting
long
narrow
spacious
thin
uncomfortable

Track 82

a   beautiful
b   delicious
c   boring
d   enjoyable
e   frightening
f   funny
g   expensive
h   interesting
i   spacious
j   narrow
k   uncomfortable

Track 83

What's the best film you've ever seen?
I don't know. What's the best film you've ever seen?

Track 84

a
Are you happy?
Yes I am. What about you?
b
Do you like chocolate?
Yes I do. Do you like chocolate?
c
Have you ever been to the North Pole?
No I haven't. Have you ever been to the North Pole?
d
Did you go to the meeting yesterday?
No, I didn't. Did you go to the meeting?

Track 85

a   Do you like your job?
b   Do you enjoy it?
c   Is it dangerous?
d   Do you have a good job?
e   Is the money good?

Track 86

MAN: Are you looking for a job?
WOMAN: Are you interested in people?
MAN: Are you good with animals?
WOMAN: Can you work in a team?
MAN: Do you like working with animals?

Track 87

MAN: Are you looking for a job? How would you like to help animals? Can you work in a team? Yes? We've got the perfect job for you. Call the Animal Hospital now! No experience required!

Track 88

How funny!
How stupid!
How silly!
How boring!
How lovely!

Track 89

a   How nice!
b   How awful!
c   How funny!
d   How boring!
e   How exciting!

Track 90

a   I have to work on Saturday.
BEEP
b   My grandfather fell and broke his leg.
BEEP
c   I'm going to Australia!
BEEP
d   Ryan got married in a Superman suit!
BEEP
e   Look, I bought you an ice cream.
BEEP

Track 91

A
What's her number?
How can I help?
Who's calling, please?
B
Is Rose there?
Do you have his number?
Can I help you?

Track 92

a   Can you help me?
b   Would you like to leave a message?
c   What time will she be back?
d   How do you spell that?
e   Do you want her to call you back?
f   Who's calling?

Track 93

a   Can I speak to Lila?
b   Are you busy?
c   Do you want me to call later?
d   When can I have it back?
e   What can I do for you?
f   How are you?

Track 94

LILA: Hello?
BEEP
LILA: Speaking.
BEEP
LILA: Fine, thanks.
BEEP

LILA: Yes, actually. I am a little.
BEEP
LILA: No, that's OK. What can I do for you?
BEEP
LILA: Oh, right. Well, I have bad news for you.

Track 95

a   We went to see my mother yesterday.
b   I don't feel like going to the party.
c   What a terrible movie.
d   She's coming to see you?
e   Take this away immediately.
f   Oh no! That's very bad news.
g   I think she's going home soon.

ANSWER KEY

Unit 1
A Listening
1 English has an official status in all the countries.
2 Matt – Australia, Sandy – Scotland,
  Wilson – Jamaica, Tessa – Canada
3 a Wilson b Tessa c Sandy d Matt e Wilson f Matt
  g Sandy h Wilson
4 a Good day
  b 33%
  c surfing, swimming
  d England, Wales, Scotland
  e Gaelic
  f Edinburgh
  g Mountains, lakes
  h Winter sports
  i Kingston
  j Music, weather
5 a east b Canadians c huge d everything e cities
  f lots g Winter
6 **Where it is:** in the Pacific Ocean
  Capital: Wellington
  Languages: English, Maori
  Most popular sports: rugby, water sports, cricket
  Interesting information: some active volcanoes
  The name of the country is New Zealand.

Unit 2
A Listening
2 a height b position c feet d understood e tall
  f sitting g teacher h class i now j work
3 *Sample answers:*
  a She is taking her exams / She has exams.
  b To make her laugh / To help her relax / To help
    with her stress.
  c No, she is still stressed / No, and she doesn't think
    the joke is funny.
4 a Don't worry, Madam, it's not hot.
  b Don't cry. It's only a joke!
  c No, just green hairy monsters with horrible faces.
  d Ten.
5 The order of the sentences is:
  9, 4, 6, 1, 5, 7, 2, 8, 3, 10

Unit 3
A Listening
1 It's a survey about television programmes / viewing
  habits.
2 **Q1:** man: 2/3 hours a day
  woman: more than 6 hours

Q2: man: documentaries
woman: soaps
Q3: man: the news
woman: documentaries
3 Man: for information ([documentaries] are interesting
  and you always learn something new).
  Woman: for fun (For me television is for fun. When I
  get home I just want to relax and have a laugh.)
5 a 1 b 2 c 1 d 2 e 2 f 2 g 2

Unit 4
A Listening
1 The show is called 'What's my job?' where people ask
  questions to guess the occupation of guests.
2 a yes b yes, sometimes c no d yes
3 a private houses, factories, subways
  b dangerous, disgusting
4 pest controller
5 a animals b kill c people d things e Pest f controller
  g pest controller h That's right
7 The correct order is: 8, 5, 4, 2, 7, 3, 1, 9. 6
8 a cabin steward on a plane

Unit 5
A Listening
1 b
2 wall, tunnel, rope ladder, tower, plank, tree house,
  wire, mud, barbed wire
3 a run b climb c drop d crawl e climb f walk
  g hang h make your way i jump j crawl
4 a run b crawl c walk along d climb e hang
  f work g jump h fall

Unit 6
A Listening
1 a Sophie b Bill c Sophie d Mandy e Mandy f Bill
  g Mandy
2 **Sophie:** She likes a romantic song that they used to
  play on the radio when she was at school, the last
  summer.
  Bill: He can't remember any particular song or
  occasion.
  Mandy: The song 'Mandy' because a boy she liked at
  school, Jerry, used to sing it in a band.
3 *Suggested answer:* What is one of the most important
  memories in your life?
4 A 2 B 4 C 3 D 1
5 a Speaker 2, referring to the sand / sea / beach.
  b Speaker 3, referring to his teacher, Mrs Taylor.

c Speaker 1, referring to the fact that she had had a baby.

d Speaker 4, referring to James, the boy she liked.

B Speaking

The correct order is F, C, A, B, D, E

Unit 7

A Listening

1 Leisure / hobbies / pastimes

2 a two

   b extreme ironing, rock climbing, canopying

3 a extreme ironing

   b an iron and an ironing board

   c ironing

   d rock climbing

   e people who enjoy life and are a bit crazy

4 a sport b iron

   c an ironing board d unusual

   e a mountain f tree g sea

   h countries i crazy

   j Extreme Ironing Offices

5 a anywhere

   b an iron and an ironing board

   c people who are a bit crazy

Unit 8

A Listening

1 The correct order is: d 1 a 2 c 3
   b 4

   a 12 o'clock (midnight)

   b She's babysitting (there are many baby things around the room)

   c She's watching TV

   d sad, probably because she is watching a sad film, and frightened by the phone calls

3 a T b F c T d T e T f T g F h F

4 b The baby was upstairs.

   g She thought it might be John, but she wasn't sure.

   h The baby was in his parents' room

5 a that you John?

   b is

   c not funny!

   d check on the

   e Please stop

   f Go

   g dropped

   h phone

   i up the stairs

   j looked

   k baby's

   l cot

   m was empty

6 a in his parents' bed

   b Mrs Donovan's brother

   c She doesn't think it's funny.

Unit 9

A Listening

1 1 picture b

   2 picture c

   3 picture f

2 **Pictures a and b:** Debbie (Peter is the caller)
   Pictures c and d: Melanie (the caller is Lucy)
   Pictures e and f: Olga and Libby (the caller is Will)

3 a Debbie b Lucy c Peter d Peter e Melanie f Will

4 a We can't take your call at the moment.

   b Please leave a message after the tone.

   c I can't come to the phone right now.

   d Leave a message and I'll ring you back.

   e We're not here right now.

5 B

B Speaking

1 a mobile phone

   b computer

   c camcorder

   d three-wheeled motorbike

   e digital camera

   f video games console

   g radio

   h MP3 player

2 a digital camera

   b camcorder

   c mobile phone

   d video games console

Unit 10

A Listening

1 **Picture A:** Chris, **Picture B:** Jezza

2 a 2 (Jezza doesn't have Chris' number on his mobile phone; he doesn't want to talk to him very much)

   b 1 (it shows Jezza isn't that bothered about him)

   c 1

   d 2 (doesn't sound like he's sure! He says 'do I believe you?')

   e difficult to tell! He says he will, but ...

3 a shows b have got c believe d want e lent f give
   g said h get i have got to

4 *Suggested answers*

   a Before, because it tells you why
      Chris lent Jezza the money.

   b He thinks office jobs are boring.

   c He is a sports lawyer.

   d He wants to be a professional DJ.

   e He wants to buy some new equipment.

5 a F b T c F d F e F

B Speaking

1 Background information
   The speaker on Track 35 is talking about a typical British Christmas celebration, where, in families, presents are put around a Christmas tree and opened sometime on December 25th.

   Picture c

Unit 11
A Listening
1   The correct order is i, a, f, g, c, h, d, e, b.
2   after
3   a m   b m   c w   d m   e w   f m   g m   h w   i w   j w
4   a   We know it's not a very nice hotel. It's dark and creepy.
   b   The man thinks he needs to protect his scared wife, but actually she's quite brave, especially when he loses his nerve. She is a bit forgetful, however.
   c   She likes tea, he likes coffee.
   d   The Exelsior hotel.
5   a isn't it?   b isn't it?   c aren't we?   d did you?
   e is it?
6   a isn't it?   b isn't it?   c didn't they?   d doesn't she?
   e is it?   f is it?   g did she?   h are they?
7   a   She thought it was dark and scary.
   b   Coffee (Charles), tea (Miranda)
   c   A seaside holiday (sun, sea, sand).
   d   She loved it.
   e   In her bag.
   f   The Hotel Excelsis.
   g   Because they had a booking there (they were actually in the wrong hotel).

Unit 12
A Listening
1   a 3   b 1   c 4   d 5   e 2
2   a   False (The Fire Service does not only fight fires.)
   b   True
   c   True
   d   False
   e   True
3   a rescue   b homeless   c owners   d volunteers
   e Clown

   a   homeless people / the homeless
   b   February 15th
   c   shoes
   d   clothes
   e   20%
   f   Tilly
   g   Trigger
   h   Dogs' and Cats' Home
   i   cats
   j   find
   k   www.dogshome.org
   l   Friends
   m   Earth
   n   sending letters
   o   making telephone calls
   p   0808 800 1111

Unit 13
A Listening
1   a   Molly – Mrs Gladwin
   b   Brian – Ms Marley
2   a G   b G   c G   d M   e M   f M   g G   h M
3   a G   b M   c M   d M   e G   f M
4   a strict   b discipline   c friendly   d wild   e ourselves
   f frighten   g attention
5   Anne d   Luke a   Pablo c   Elsa b
6   a   She was shy, with long hair down to her waist.
   b   She used to go red.
   c   She played the violin.
   d   Pablo
   e   He had gorgeous dark eyes, long eye lashes, curly hair, and a cheeky smile.
   f   He used to make animal noises.
   g   He had short hair and his eyes were close together.
   h   No (she calls him 'horrible').
B Speaking
1   1 c   2 f   3 d   4 e   5 b   6 g   7 h   8 a
2   1, 2, 3, 4, 5, 7, 8 (all except 6)

Unit 14
A Listening
1   airport, car crash, dog, egg, prime minister, queen, student, tower, the environment, nurses
2   airport (Mike Gartside), car crash, nurses (Antonia Merritt),
   dog (Phyllis Jones), egg, the environment (Stephen Williams),
   prime minister (Stephen Williams), queen (Antonia Merritt),
   student (Mark Gartside), tower (Stephen Williams)
3   a   Phyllis Jones' dog
   b   Mark Gartside
   c   Stephen Williams
   d   Phyllis Jones
   e   Antonia Merritt
   f   the Prime Minister
   g   Stephen Williams
   h   Antonia Merritt
   i   Phyllis Jones
   j   the Prime Minister
   k   Antonia Merritt
   l   Mark Gartside
4   a   42
   b   an egg
   c   protesting
   d   environment
   e   laughed
   f   21
   g   architecture
   h   airport
   i   sea
   j   87
   k   floor

l heard
m problem
n life

B Speaking
1 a Building 3
   b Building 2
   c Building 4
   d Building 1
2 Building 2

Unit 15
A Listening
2 1c 2f 3e 4d 5a 6d
3 a Tricia b Marty c Marty
   d Marty
4 a 1 b 3 c 2 d 4 e 5 f 2
5 a Down and to the right
   b Directly to the right
   c Directly to the left
   d Up and to the left
   e Up and to the right
   f Down and to the left

Unit 16
A Listening
1 UFOs
2
Picture A
a 6 b 5 c 4 d 1 e 2 f 3
Picture B
a 4 b 1 c 6 d 2 e 5 f 3
3
Picture A
a 1 b 3 c 2 d 3 e 2 f 1 g 2
Picture B
a 3 b 2 c 1 d 1 e 3 f 2 g3
B Speaking
1 a He wanted company
   b his twin brother, Kevin

Pronunciation Exercises 1
A: Sounds
1 1 television 2 conclusion 3 usual 4 decision
   5 information 6 solution 7 obsession 8 fashion
2 Words with /ʒ/ sound: television, conclusion, usual,
   decision
   Words with /ʃ/ sound: information, solution, obsession,
   fashion
3 /ʃ/ sugar, solution, fashion, discussion
   /ʒ/ usually, conclusion, television, decision
5 /ɒ/ cop – clock, drop, opposite, top;
   /æ/ cap – Amelie, back, hang, ladder, plank, platform;
   /ʌ/ cup – front, jump, mud, someone (X 2), son, tunnel,
   under
6 a /e/ check
   b /ei/ train
   c /ei/ plane
   d /e/ left
   e /e/ get
   f /ei/ bay
   g /ei/ take
   h /ei/ say
   i /e/ then
   j /e/ better
   k /ei/ gate
7 a sin 8
   b sing 1
   c tonne 5
   d tongue 10
   e ran 12
   f rang 11
   g sun 6
   h sung 7
   i sinner 3
   j singer 4
   k thin 9
   l thing 2

/n/ sound as in none: sin, tonne, ran, sun, sinner, thin

/ŋ/ as in long: sing, tongue, singer, rang, sung, thing
8 bingo 1 drink 5 fun 6 no 3 sound 4
   sun 7 sung 8 swimming 2 thin 10 thing 11
   think 12 thanks 9
9 /n/: fun, no, sound, sun, thin
   /ŋ/: bingo, swimming, drink, sung, thanks, thing,
   think
10 The sound /n/ can go at the beginning, in the middle
    and at the end of words.
    The sound /ŋ/ can go in the middle and at the end of
    words but it cannot go at the beginning.
11 a free b tank('s) c parts d north e theme f sings
    g think h dirty i first
12 three, thank, path, north, theme,
    things, think, thirty, thirst

13 /θ/: thank, with, three, north, thirty, mouth
/ð/: that, mother, father, this

15, 16
  a /aʊ/ town
  b /aʊ/ round
  c /əʊ/ bone
  d /əʊ/ phone
  e /əʊ/ clone
  f /aʊ/ clown
  g /əʊ/ tone
  h /aʊ/ house
  i /əʊ/ moan
  j /aʊ/ down

17 a 2
    1
  b 1
    2
  c 1
    2
  d 2
    1

18 a b 2 **b** a 2 **c** d 2 **d** d 2 **e** b 1 **f** a 1
  g c 1 **h** c 2

19 There are two different ways of pronouncing the soelling 'ei':

20 a /ai/ **b** /iː/ **c** /iː/ **d** /ai/ **e** /ai/ **f** /iː/

21 a S **b** D **c** D **d** S **e** D **f** S

22 a (/gəˈrɑːʒ/) /ˈgærɪdʒ/
    (/gəˈrɑːʒ/) /ˈgærɪdʒ/
  b /gəˈrɑːʒ/ (/ˈgærɪdʒ/)
    (/gəˈrɑːʒ/) /ˈgærɪdʒ/
  c (/ruːm/) /rʊm/
    /ruːm/ (/rʊm/)
  d (/ruːm/) /rʊm/
    (/ruːm/) /rʊm/
  e (/nuː/) /njuː/
    /nuː/ (/njuː/)
  f /nuː/ (/njuː/)
    /nuː/ (/njuː/)

23 UFO is pronounced as individual letters.
AIDS is pronounced as a word.

24 a BBC **b** USA **c** BLT **d** OPEC
  e UN, UNICEF **f** UK **g** DVD

25 a Unidentified Flying Object
  b Digital Video Disc
  c British Broadcasting Corporation
  d United States of America

26 a UFO
  b DVD
  c BBC
  d USA

Pronunciation Exercises 2

B: Stress

1, 2, 3
The stress goes on the first word in every case.

5 Shape 1: healthy, diet, massage, lifestyle, problem
  Shape 2: explain, accept, complete

7 Shape 1: coffee, chocolate, water, salad, practise
  Shape 2: inside, without

8 a can (strong – beginning of the sentence), can (strong – short answer), can (weak within a sentence, not stressed)
  b was (weak – within the sentence, not stressed), and (strong – stressed), was (weak – not stressed), and (weak – not stressed)
  c was (strong – stressed at the beginning of the sentence), was (strong – short answer, stressed), was (weak), was (weak)

9 a was [S], was [W], and [W],
  b can [S], can [S], can [W],
  c was [W], was [W], and [W], was [S], was [W], and [S]

12 1 going to, 2 gonna

13 a 1 **b** 2 **c** 1, 1 **d** 2, 2

14 a We're gonna <u>go</u> to the beach.
  b She's <u>going</u> to win.
  c <u>James</u> is going to study French.
  d <u>They're</u> gonna tell you to stop.

16 One syllable
bad, cheap, cramped, deep, fast, fat, good, high, long, thin
Two syllables
ugly, boring, frightening, funny, narrow, spacious
Three syllables
beautiful, delicious, horrible, expensive,
Four syllables
enjoyable, uncomfortable, interesting

17 a beautiful ■□□
  b delicious □■□
  c boring ■□
  d enjoyable □■□□
  e frightening ■□□
  f funny ■□
  g expensive □■□
  h interesting ■□□
  i spacious ■□
  j narrow ■□
  k uncomfortable □■□□

18 What's the <u>best</u> film you've ever seen?
I don't know. What's the best film <u>you've</u> ever seen?

19 The stress is on the words:
  a Are, am, you **b** chocolate **c** you, No **d** No, you

Pronunciation Exercises 3

C: Intonation

1   No change

2
The voice goes up at the end of the
questions.

3   'How would you like to help animals?' has a falling
intonation; it goes down at the end.

4   a, e I
b, c, d B

6   *Suggested answers*
a   How boring!
b   How awful!
c   How exciting!
d   How funny!
e   How nice!

7   a   questions are all Wh questions.
b   questions are Yes / No questions.

8   a   Wh' questions = falling
intonation;
b   Yes / No questions = rising intonation

9   a   up
b   up
c   down
d   down
e   up
f   down

11 a up   b up   c up   d down   e down   f down

13 a   Can I speak to Lila?
b   How are you?
c   Are you busy?
d   Do you want me to call back
later?
e   When can I have it back?

14 a   happy
b   sad
c   bored
d   surprised
e   angry
f   upset
g   tired

Audio reference list

CD 1		CD 2		
Track		Track		
1	2:44	1	47	2:05
2	0:41	2	48	0:19
3	0:49	3	49	0:28
4	1:02	4	50	0:38
5	1:07	5	51	0:42
6	0:31	6	52	0:49
7	0:50	7	53	0:24
8	0:43	8	54	0:54
9	1:14	9	55	0:35
10	1:34	10	56	0:57
11	1:17	11	57	0:44
12	2:07	12	57	0:28
13	1:05	13	59	0:07
14	1:33	14	60	0:38
15	0:10	15	61	0:57
16	2:24	16	62	0:13
17	2:02	17	63	0:30
18	1:30	18	64	0:46
19	1:58	19	65	0:14
20	2:19	20	66	0:42
21	1:14	21	67	2:04
22	3:00	22	68	0:18
23	2:08	23	69	0:33
24	2:31	24	70	0:48
25	0:38	25	71	0:13
26	1:53	26	72	0:36
27	1:55	27	73	0:15
28	0:32	28	74	0:53
29	0:37	29	75	0:28
30	1:08	30	76	0:30
31	1:19	31	77	0:40
32	1:30	32	78	0:09
33	1:02	33	79	0:26
34	0:34	34	80	0:21
35	0:50	35	81	1:32
36	2:48	36	82	1:19
37	2:40	37	83	0:11
38	1:24	38	84	0:32
39	2:00	39	85	0:24
40	1:34	40	86	0:17
41	1:44	41	87	0:18
42	2:00	42	88	0:18
43	1:15	43	89	0:35
44	2:36	44	90	0:47
45	3:38	45	91	0:20
46	2:59	46	92	0:27
		47	93	0:42
		48	94	0:46
		49	95	0:38